THE MINDFUL ENTREPRENEUR:

BUILDING A SUCCESSFUL BUSINESS THROUGH MEDITATION

PATRICK K. THIGPEN

Table of contents

Preface...**4**

Chapter 1: Introduction to Mindful Entrepreneurship. 7

Defining Mindful Entrepreneurship........................... 7

Benefits Of Integrating Meditation With Business.....8

Chapter 2: Cultivating Mindfulness for Business Success.. **11**

Understanding Mindfulness and its Relevance to Entrepreneurship.. 11

Techniques for Developing Mindfulness in Daily Life.. 12

Chapter 3: The Entrepreneur's Mind: Enhancing Awareness and Focus..**15**

Practicing Meditation for Improved Self-Awareness and Concentration.. 15

Strategies to Enhance Focus and Productivity in Business Endeavors.. 16

Chapter 4: Managing Stress and Embracing Uncertainty...**19**

Utilizing Meditation to Cope with Stress and Uncertainty...19

Building Resilience and Adaptability in Entrepreneurial Pursuits... 20

Chapter 5: Decision-Making and Intuition: Trusting Your Inner Guide..**23**

Developing Intuitive Decision-Making Skills through Mindfulness Practices..23

Applying Mindfulness Techniques to Make Conscious and Informed Choices..........................24

Chapter 6: Nurturing Creativity and Innovation.......27

Unleashing Creative Thinking through Meditation and Mindfulness...27

Using Mindfulness to Overcome Creative Blocks and Foster Innovation...29

Chapter 7: Work-Life Integration: Balancing Entrepreneurship and Well-being............................. 32

Creating Harmony between Work and Personal Life through Mindfulness.. 32

Techniques for Maintaining Work-Life Balance and Preventing Burnout.. 34

Chapter 8: Effective Communication and Building Relationships.. 37

Enhancing Communication Skills through Mindful Listening and Empathy... 37

Cultivating Meaningful Connections and Collaborations in Business.................................... 39

Chapter 9: Mindful Leadership: Inspiring and Empowering Others...42

Integrating Mindfulness into Leadership Practices. 42

Becoming a Mindful Leader Who Inspires and Motivates Teams..44

Chapter 10: Sustaining Growth and Resilience.......47

Cultivating a Growth Mindset and Resilience through Meditation.. 47

Overcoming Setbacks, Learning from Failures, and Embracing Growth Opportunities...........................49

Conclusion.. 52

Preface

Welcome to "The Mindful Entrepreneur: Building a Successful Business Through Meditation." In today's fast-paced and competitive business world, the journey of entrepreneurship can be both exhilarating and challenging. As entrepreneurs, we often find ourselves constantly striving for success, chasing goals, and navigating through the complexities of building and growing a business.

Amidst this whirlwind, it is easy to lose sight of our well-being, inner balance, and the purpose behind our entrepreneurial endeavors. We may sacrifice our health, relationships, and even our own happiness in the pursuit of achievement. But what if there is a different path—one that embraces both success and mindfulness, where we can build thriving businesses while nurturing our own well-being?

This book aims to bridge the gap between the entrepreneurial spirit and the practice of mindfulness. It explores the profound potential of incorporating meditation into our business lives—how it can transform not only our professional endeavors but also our personal growth and overall sense of fulfillment.

Drawing from ancient wisdom traditions and modern scientific research, "The Mindful Entrepreneur" invites you on a journey to discover the transformative power of mindfulness in entrepreneurship. It offers practical insights, techniques, and real-life examples to help you cultivate a mindset that combines focus, clarity, resilience, and compassion in your entrepreneurial pursuits.

Each chapter in this book is designed to explore different aspects of mindful entrepreneurship, providing you with tools and practices that can be integrated seamlessly into your daily routine. Through meditation and mindfulness, you will learn to enhance your decision-making abilities, manage stress, nurture creativity, and foster meaningful relationships with others.

But this book is not just about business success; it is about creating a balanced and purposeful life as an entrepreneur. It acknowledges that true success encompasses not only financial achievements but also personal growth, well-being, and a positive impact on the world around us.

As the author, I have personally experienced the transformative power of mindfulness in my own entrepreneurial journey. I have witnessed the positive filled with distractions and constant demands, the ability to stay present and focused on the task at hand becomes a competitive advantage. By training the mind through meditation, entrepreneurs can improve their ability to concentrate, make clear decisions, and execute plans with greater efficiency.

Moreover, meditation cultivates resilience and emotional well-being. The entrepreneurial journey is often accompanied by stress, uncertainty, and setbacks. Meditation provides entrepreneurs with the tools to navigate these challenges with grace and equanimity. Regular meditation practice reduces stress levels, improves emotional regulation, and enhances overall well-being, enabling entrepreneurs to approach difficulties with a calm and balanced mindset.

In addition, integrating meditation with business can foster a compassionate and ethical business culture. Mindful entrepreneurs recognize the interconnectedness of all beings and strive to create businesses that prioritize the well-being of employees, customers, and the broader community. By practicing meditation and cultivating compassion, entrepreneurs can develop a deep sense of responsibility and make decisions that align with their values, fostering a positive and sustainable impact on society.

In conclusion, mindful entrepreneurship combines the principles of mindfulness with the mindset and practices of entrepreneurship. It emphasizes self-awareness, conscious decision-making, and the cultivation of a compassionate and ethical business culture. By integrating meditation practices into the entrepreneurial journey, individuals can enhance their self-awareness, concentration, resilience, and emotional well-being. Mindful entrepreneurship offers numerous benefits that not only contribute to the success of businesses but also promote the well-being of individuals and society as a whole.

changes it brings not only to my business but also to my relationships, health, and overall happiness. I am excited to share these insights with you and to guide you on this unique path of mindful entrepreneurship.

"The Mindful Entrepreneur" is an invitation for you to embark on a remarkable journey—a journey that integrates the principles of mindfulness into the fabric of your business and your life. It is my hope that this book will inspire and empower you to build a successful business while remaining true to your values, nurturing your well-being, and making a meaningful difference in the world.

I encourage you to approach this book with an open mind and a willingness to explore new possibilities. Embrace the practices and concepts presented here, adapt them to your own unique circumstances, and observe the profound impact they can have on your entrepreneurial path.

May this book serve as a guiding light, illuminating your way to becoming a mindful entrepreneur—a visionary leader who not only achieves great success but also creates a more conscious and compassionate world through the business you build.

Chapter 1: Introduction to Mindful Entrepreneurship

In recent years, there has been a growing recognition of the importance of mindfulness in various aspects of life, including the realm of entrepreneurship. Mindful entrepreneurship is a concept that combines the principles of mindfulness with the mindset and practices of entrepreneurship. It involves applying the principles of presence, awareness, and compassion to the process of starting and running a business.

Defining Mindful Entrepreneurship

We can say that it is an approach to entrepreneurship that emphasizes self-awareness, conscious decision-making, and the cultivation of a compassionate and ethical business culture. It involves developing a deep understanding of oneself, as well as the impact of one's actions on others and the environment. Mindful entrepreneurs strive to create businesses that not only generate profits but also contribute to the well-being of employees, customers, and society as a whole.

One of the key aspects of mindful entrepreneurship is the integration of meditation practices into the business routine. Meditation, in its various forms, has been practiced for centuries as a means of cultivating mindfulness and inner peace. By incorporating meditation into the entrepreneurial journey, individuals can enhance their ability to stay present, focused, and resilient in the face of challenges.

Benefits Of Integrating Meditation With Business

The benefits of integrating meditation with business are numerous and profound. Firstly, meditation helps entrepreneurs develop a heightened sense of self-awareness. Through regular practice, entrepreneurs become more attuned to their thoughts, emotions, and bodily sensations, allowing them to make conscious decisions based on a deeper understanding of themselves and their values. This self-awareness also extends to their interactions with others, fostering better communication, empathy, and conflict resolution skills.

Secondly, meditation enhances concentration and focus, which are crucial qualities for entrepreneurs. In a world

Chapter 2: Cultivating Mindfulness for Business Success

In Chapter 1, we explored the concept of mindful entrepreneurship and the benefits of integrating meditation with business. Building upon that foundation, Chapter 2 delves deeper into the practice of mindfulness and provides techniques for cultivating mindfulness in daily life to enhance business success.

Understanding Mindfulness and its Relevance to Entrepreneurship

Understanding mindfulness and its relevance to entrepreneurship is essential for entrepreneurs seeking to harness its power. Mindfulness is the practice of paying attention to the present moment with non-judgmental awareness. It involves fully engaging with the task at hand, observing thoughts and emotions without getting caught up in them, and accepting things as they are.

For entrepreneurs, mindfulness is particularly relevant due to the fast-paced and demanding nature of the business world. It enables individuals to stay focused, make clear decisions, and respond effectively to challenges. By cultivating mindfulness, entrepreneurs can develop a greater sense of clarity, creativity, and resilience, allowing them to navigate the complexities of business with greater ease and success.

Techniques for Developing Mindfulness in Daily Life

To develop mindfulness in daily life, entrepreneurs can employ various techniques that help cultivate present-moment awareness and foster a state of mindfulness. Here are a few techniques that can be particularly beneficial:

1. Mindful Breathing: The breath is an anchor that can bring us back to the present moment. By focusing on the sensations of the breath—feeling the air enter and leave the body—entrepreneurs can cultivate a sense of grounding and presence. Taking a few moments throughout the day to focus on the breath can help center the mind and reduce stress.

2. Body Scan: The body scan is a practice that involves systematically directing attention to different parts of the body, noticing sensations without judgment. This technique promotes awareness of bodily sensations and helps entrepreneurs develop a deeper connection with their physical experience, fostering a sense of embodiment and groundedness.

3. Mindful Walking: Walking mindfully involves paying attention to the sensations of each step, feeling the contact of the feet with the ground, and observing the movement of the body. Engaging in mindful walking during breaks or as a transition between tasks can bring a sense of calm and presence to the entrepreneurial journey.

4. Daily Mindfulness Rituals: Incorporating mindfulness into daily routines can be transformative. Simple activities like mindful eating, brushing teeth, or washing dishes can become opportunities for practicing presence and awareness. By fully immersing oneself in these routine tasks, entrepreneurs can train the mind to be more focused and attentive in all aspects of life.

5. Formal Meditation Practice: Setting aside dedicated time for formal meditation practice is an invaluable way to deepen mindfulness. Whether it's through mindfulness meditation, loving-kindness meditation, or other techniques, regular meditation practice allows entrepreneurs to cultivate a state of heightened awareness, clarity, and emotional well-being.

Incorporating these techniques into daily life may initially require effort and discipline. However, with consistent practice, entrepreneurs can develop a natural and effortless state of mindfulness, enhancing their ability to thrive in the entrepreneurial realm.

By cultivating mindfulness, entrepreneurs gain the capacity to respond to challenges with wisdom and equanimity. They develop a heightened awareness of their own thoughts, emotions, and behaviors, enabling them to make conscious decisions and navigate the complexities of business more effectively.

Chapter 3: The Entrepreneur's Mind: Enhancing Awareness and Focus

In Chapter 2, we explored the cultivation of mindfulness in daily life. Building upon that foundation, Chapter 3 delves deeper into the development of an entrepreneur's mind by focusing on enhancing awareness and improving concentration. This chapter explores the power of meditation as a tool for self-awareness and concentration and provides strategies to enhance focus and productivity in business endeavors.

Practicing Meditation for Improved Self-Awareness and Concentration

Meditation is a powerful practice for entrepreneurs to cultivate self-awareness and enhance concentration. By regularly dedicating time to meditation, entrepreneurs can train their minds to become more present and focused, resulting in a heightened level of awareness and concentration in their daily activities. Here are a few meditation techniques that can be particularly beneficial:

a. Mindfulness Meditation: Mindfulness meditation involves bringing attention to the present moment, observing thoughts, emotions, and sensations without judgment. By practicing mindfulness meditation, entrepreneurs can develop a deep understanding of their thought patterns, emotional reactions, and habitual behaviors. This self-awareness allows for greater clarity and conscious decision-making in business.

b. Concentration Meditation: Concentration meditation involves focusing the attention on a single object, such as the breath or a specific visualization. Through the cultivation of concentration, entrepreneurs can strengthen their ability to sustain attention and resist distractions. This practice enhances focus and trains the mind to stay present with the task at hand, leading to improved productivity and efficiency.

Strategies to Enhance Focus and Productivity in Business Endeavors

In addition to meditation, there are several strategies entrepreneurs can employ to enhance focus and productivity in their business endeavors:

a. Prioritize and Set Clear Goals: Clear prioritization and goal-setting are essential for maintaining focus. By identifying the most important tasks and setting specific goals, entrepreneurs can direct their attention and energy towards activities that align with their objectives. Breaking down larger goals into smaller, manageable tasks also helps in maintaining focus and progress.

b. Create a Distraction-Free Environment: Minimizing distractions is crucial for improving focus. Entrepreneurs can create a designated workspace free from unnecessary interruptions and distractions. This can involve turning off notifications on electronic devices, utilizing time-blocking techniques, or even finding a quiet physical space conducive to concentration.

c. Practice Time Management: Effective time management is vital for optimizing productivity. Entrepreneurs can utilize techniques such as the Pomodoro Technique, where work is divided into focused intervals followed by short breaks. By structuring their time, entrepreneurs can make the most of their energy and maintain sustained focus on their tasks.

d. Cultivate Single-Tasking: Multitasking can often lead to reduced productivity and scattered attention. Cultivating the practice of single-tasking involves dedicating full attention to one task at a time. By focusing on a single task without distractions, entrepreneurs can deepen their concentration and accomplish tasks more efficiently.

e. Take Regular Breaks: Rest and rejuvenation are essential for maintaining focus and productivity. Entrepreneurs should incorporate regular breaks into their work schedule, allowing time for relaxation, movement, and renewal. Short breaks can help recharge the mind, prevent burnout, and enhance overall mental clarity.

By integrating these strategies into their entrepreneurial journey, entrepreneurs can enhance their focus, productivity, and overall success. Mindfulness meditation acts as a foundation for cultivating self-awareness and concentration, while implementing specific strategies supports the development of effective work habits and a focused mindset.

Chapter 4: Managing Stress and Embracing Uncertainty

Chapter 4 delves into the critical topic of managing stress and embracing uncertainty, two common challenges faced by entrepreneurs. This chapter focuses on the utilization of meditation as a tool to cope with stress and uncertainty and emphasizes the importance of building resilience and adaptability in entrepreneurial pursuits.

Utilizing Meditation to Cope with Stress and Uncertainty

Entrepreneurship often involves high levels of stress and uncertainty. The ability to manage these challenges is crucial for maintaining well-being and making sound decisions. Meditation provides valuable techniques for coping with stress and embracing uncertainty:

a. Mindfulness-Based Stress Reduction (MBSR): MBSR is a structured program that combines mindfulness meditation, body awareness, and gentle movement. By practicing MBSR, entrepreneurs can cultivate a non-reactive awareness of stressful thoughts and emotions, allowing them to respond to stressors with greater clarity and resilience.

b. Loving-Kindness Meditation: Loving-kindness meditation involves generating feelings of love, compassion, and goodwill towards oneself and others. This practice promotes emotional well-being, reduces negative self-talk, and cultivates a sense of interconnectedness. By embracing loving-kindness meditation, entrepreneurs can navigate stressful situations with a compassionate and empathetic mindset.

c. Acceptance and Letting Go: Meditation encourages the practice of acceptance and letting go, which is particularly relevant in the face of uncertainty. Entrepreneurs can learn to acknowledge and accept the uncertainties inherent in their entrepreneurial journey, releasing attachment to specific outcomes. This mindset allows for greater adaptability and the ability to navigate uncertainty with grace.

Building Resilience and Adaptability in Entrepreneurial Pursuits

Resilience and adaptability are essential qualities for entrepreneurs to effectively navigate the ups and downs of their journey. Here are strategies to build resilience and adaptability:

a. Embrace a Growth Mindset: Cultivating a growth mindset involves viewing challenges and failures as opportunities for learning and growth. Entrepreneurs can reframe setbacks as valuable lessons and use them as stepping stones towards improvement and success. This mindset promotes resilience and fosters a positive attitude towards uncertainty.

b. Foster a Supportive Network: Building a supportive network of mentors, peers, and like-minded individuals provides entrepreneurs with a valuable source of support and guidance. Collaborating and connecting with others in the entrepreneurial community allows for shared experiences and learning from one another's resilience and adaptability.

c. Practice Self-Care: Taking care of one's physical and mental well-being is crucial for building resilience. Entrepreneurs should prioritize self-care practices such as regular exercise, proper nutrition, quality sleep, and leisure activities that promote relaxation and rejuvenation. A healthy and balanced lifestyle enhances overall resilience and adaptability.

d. Develop Problem-Solving Skills: Developing strong problem-solving skills equips entrepreneurs with the ability to navigate challenges and find solutions. By honing their critical thinking, decision-making, and creativity, entrepreneurs can approach uncertainties with confidence and resourcefulness.

e. Stay Flexible and Open-Minded: Embracing uncertainty requires flexibility and open-mindedness. Entrepreneurs should be willing to adapt their strategies, embrace new ideas, and pivot when necessary. By remaining open to change and being flexible in their approach, entrepreneurs can respond effectively to the ever-changing business landscape.

By utilizing meditation practices to cope with stress and uncertainty and implementing strategies to build resilience and adaptability, entrepreneurs can navigate the entrepreneurial journey with greater ease and succes

Chapter 5: Decision-Making and Intuition: Trusting Your Inner Guide

In Chapter 4, we explored managing stress and embracing uncertainty in entrepreneurship. This chapter delves into the realm of decision-making and intuition, highlighting the importance of developing intuitive decision-making skills through mindfulness practices. This chapter emphasizes the application of mindfulness techniques to make conscious and informed choices in the entrepreneurial journey.

Developing Intuitive Decision-Making Skills through Mindfulness Practices

Intuition is a valuable resource for entrepreneurs, providing insights and guidance that can lead to more effective decision-making. Mindfulness practices can help entrepreneurs develop and trust their intuition by cultivating a heightened sense of awareness and presence. Here are some mindfulness techniques that facilitate the development of intuitive decision-making skills:

a. Body Awareness: Mindfulness involves bringing attention to bodily sensations. By cultivating body awareness, entrepreneurs can tune into the subtle physical signals and cues that accompany different decisions. The body often provides valuable information and insights that can guide intuitive decision-making.

b. Mindful Inquiry: Mindful inquiry involves investigating thoughts, emotions, and beliefs with curiosity and non-judgment. By exploring the underlying motivations and biases behind decision options, entrepreneurs can gain clarity and make choices that align with their values and long-term goals.

c. Silent Reflection: Taking moments of silent reflection before making decisions allows entrepreneurs to tap into their intuitive wisdom. By creating a space of stillness and quieting the mind, entrepreneurs can access deeper insights and gut feelings that may guide them towards the most appropriate choices.

Applying Mindfulness Techniques to Make Conscious and Informed Choices

Mindfulness techniques can be directly applied to the decision-making process, enabling entrepreneurs to make conscious and informed choices. Here are some ways to integrate mindfulness into the decision-making process:

a. Present-Moment Awareness: Mindfulness emphasizes being fully present in the moment. By bringing awareness to the present moment, entrepreneurs can focus their attention on gathering relevant information, considering different perspectives, and assessing the potential impact of their decisions.

b. Non-Attachment to Outcomes: Mindfulness encourages non-attachment to specific outcomes. By letting go of rigid expectations and surrendering to the uncertainty of outcomes, entrepreneurs can make decisions with a sense of openness and flexibility. This approach allows for greater adaptability and the ability to pivot when necessary.

c. Cultivating Equanimity: Equanimity is the ability to remain balanced and calm in the face of uncertainty and challenges. By cultivating equanimity through mindfulness, entrepreneurs can make decisions from a place of inner stability and clarity, free from reactive emotions that may cloud judgment.

d. Mindful Evaluation: Mindful evaluation involves objectively assessing the pros and cons of different options while remaining aware of personal biases and preferences. By carefully examining the potential risks, rewards, and consequences, entrepreneurs can make more informed and balanced decisions.

e. Trusting Intuition: Mindfulness helps entrepreneurs develop trust in their intuition. By honoring and valuing their intuitive insights, entrepreneurs can integrate their logical analysis with intuitive wisdom to make decisions that align with their authentic selves and long-term vision.

By applying mindfulness techniques to the decision-making process, entrepreneurs can make conscious and informed choices that draw upon both rational analysis and intuitive insights.

Chapter 6: Nurturing Creativity and Innovation

Chapter 6 explores the realm of nurturing creativity and fostering innovation in entrepreneurship. It highlights the power of meditation and mindfulness in unleashing creative thinking, overcoming creative blocks, and cultivating an innovative mindset.

Unleashing Creative Thinking through Meditation and Mindfulness

Meditation and mindfulness practices can serve as catalysts for unleashing creative thinking in entrepreneurs. By cultivating a present-moment awareness and a non-judgmental mindset, entrepreneurs can tap into their innate creativity. Here are some ways meditation and mindfulness can facilitate creative thinking:

a. Cultivating Curiosity: Mindfulness encourages a state of curiosity and open-mindedness. By approaching thoughts, emotions, and experiences with a sense of curiosity, entrepreneurs can unlock new perspectives and fresh insights that fuel creative thinking.

b. Breaking Patterns: Meditation and mindfulness help entrepreneurs break free from habitual thought patterns and conditioned responses. By observing thoughts without judgment and letting go of preconceived notions, entrepreneurs can create space for innovative ideas and solutions to emerge.

c. Accessing the Subconscious Mind: Meditation can provide access to the subconscious mind, where creativity often resides. Through practices such as visualization, loving-kindness meditation, or deep relaxation techniques, entrepreneurs can tap into their deeper layers of creativity and intuition.

d. Enhancing Divergent Thinking: Mindfulness practices stimulate divergent thinking, which involves generating multiple ideas and possibilities. By expanding awareness and letting go of self-imposed limitations, entrepreneurs can access their creative potential and explore novel solutions to business challenges.

Using Mindfulness to Overcome Creative Blocks and Foster Innovation

Creative blocks can hinder the flow of ideas and innovation. Mindfulness can be instrumental in overcoming these blocks and fostering a mindset conducive to innovation. Here's how mindfulness techniques can help:

a. Embracing Uncertainty: Innovation often involves venturing into the unknown. Mindfulness teaches entrepreneurs to embrace uncertainty and let go of the need for immediate solutions. By cultivating a mindset of openness and curiosity, entrepreneurs can explore uncharted territories and discover innovative ideas.

b. Managing Fear and Self-Doubt: Fear and self-doubt can stifle creativity. Mindfulness practices enable entrepreneurs to observe these thoughts and emotions without judgment, reducing their power over creative expression. By developing self-compassion and a non-judgmental mindset, entrepreneurs can overcome fear and self-doubt, creating a nurturing environment for innovation.

c. Cultivating Playfulness and Playful Mindset: Playfulness is closely linked to creativity and innovation. Mindfulness techniques encourage entrepreneurs to approach their work with a playful mindset, allowing them to explore unconventional ideas and take risks. By embracing a sense of play and experimentation, entrepreneurs can ignite their creative spark and unlock innovative solutions.

d. Fostering Connection and Collaboration: Mindfulness practices enhance interpersonal connection and empathy, fostering an environment of collaboration and collective creativity. By actively listening, appreciating diverse perspectives, and practicing mindful communication, entrepreneurs can tap into the collective wisdom of their team and generate innovative ideas together.

This chapter emphasizes the power of meditation and mindfulness in nurturing creativity and fostering innovation. By integrating these practices, entrepreneurs can unleash their creative potential, overcome blocks, and cultivate an innovative mindset. Through curiosity, openness, and a playful approach, entrepreneurs can bring forth new ideas, products, and services that push the boundaries of their entrepreneurial endeavors.

Chapter 7: Work-Life Integration: Balancing Entrepreneurship and Well-being

We will delve into the important topic of work-life integration and explore how mindfulness can help entrepreneurs create harmony between their work and personal life. It emphasizes the significance of maintaining work-life balance and offers techniques to prevent burnout and nurture overall well-being.

Creating Harmony between Work and Personal Life through Mindfulness

Mindfulness practices provide entrepreneurs with valuable tools to create harmony between their work and personal life. By cultivating present-moment awareness and non-judgmental acceptance, entrepreneurs can navigate the demands of entrepreneurship while prioritizing their well-being. Here's how mindfulness can support work-life integration:

a. Setting Boundaries: Mindfulness helps entrepreneurs establish clear boundaries between work and personal life. By consciously designating specific times for work, relaxation, and quality time with loved ones, entrepreneurs can create a balanced schedule that honors both professional and personal commitments.

b. Practicing Presence: Mindfulness encourages entrepreneurs to be fully present in each moment, whether at work or engaging in personal activities. By giving undivided attention to the present moment, entrepreneurs can fully engage in their work tasks and personal experiences, enhancing focus, satisfaction, and overall well-being.

c. Cultivating Gratitude: Mindfulness practices promote the cultivation of gratitude. By regularly acknowledging and appreciating the positive aspects of both work and personal life, entrepreneurs can foster a sense of fulfillment and contentment. This gratitude mindset supports work-life integration by creating a positive outlook on all aspects of life.

d. Embracing Flexibility: Mindfulness allows entrepreneurs to cultivate flexibility and adaptability. By remaining open to change and adjusting their plans when necessary, entrepreneurs can respond to the evolving demands of work and personal life. This adaptability fosters a sense of balance and reduces stress associated with rigid expectations.

Techniques for Maintaining Work-Life Balance and Preventing Burnout

Maintaining work-life balance is crucial for preventing burnout and nurturing overall well-being. Here are some techniques that entrepreneurs can employ to prioritize self-care and maintain work-life balance:

a. Time Management: Effective time management is key to maintaining work-life balance. Entrepreneurs can utilize techniques such as prioritizing tasks, delegating responsibilities, and establishing efficient workflows. By optimizing their use of time, entrepreneurs can allocate dedicated periods for work and personal activities.

b. Regular Self-Care Practices: Self-care is vital for preventing burnout and nurturing well-being. Entrepreneurs should prioritize self-care practices such as exercise, meditation, hobbies, spending time with loved ones, and engaging in activities that bring joy and relaxation. Regular self-care helps recharge energy levels and promotes overall work-life balance.

c. Learning to Delegate: Entrepreneurs often wear many hats, but it's essential to delegate tasks and responsibilities to maintain balance. Delegating allows entrepreneurs to focus on their core strengths and passions while empowering team members to contribute their skills and expertise. Effective delegation helps prevent overwhelm and promotes a healthier work-life integration.

d. Creating Tech Boundaries: Technology can blur the lines between work and personal life. Establishing boundaries with technology, such as setting specific times for checking emails or turning off notifications during personal time, helps create space for relaxation, leisure, and quality time with loved ones.

e. Regular Reflection and Evaluation: Taking regular moments for reflection and evaluation enables entrepreneurs to assess their work-life balance and make necessary adjustments. Mindful reflection allows entrepreneurs to check in with their well-being, identify areas of imbalance, and take proactive steps to restore equilibrium.

Chapter 7 emphasizes the importance of work-life integration and offers techniques for maintaining work-life balance and preventing burnout. By incorporating mindfulness practices, setting boundaries, prioritizing self-care, and cultivating flexibility, entrepreneurs can create a harmonious integration of work and personal life. This integration promotes overall well-being, satisfaction, and sustainable success in the entrepreneurial journey.

Chapter 8: Effective Communication and Building Relationships

Chapter 8 explores the crucial aspects of effective communication and building strong relationships in the realm of entrepreneurship. It highlights the significance of enhancing communication skills through mindful listening and empathy, as well as cultivating meaningful connections and collaborations in business.

Enhancing Communication Skills through Mindful Listening and Empathy

Effective communication is a cornerstone of successful entrepreneurship. Mindfulness practices offer valuable techniques for enhancing communication skills, fostering deeper connections, and promoting understanding. Here's how mindfulness can improve communication:

a. Mindful Listening: Mindful listening involves giving full attention to the speaker without judgment or interruption. By practicing mindful listening, entrepreneurs can cultivate a deep presence and understanding, which leads to clearer communication, improved problem-solving, and stronger relationships.

b. Non-Verbal Awareness: Mindfulness encourages entrepreneurs to pay attention to non-verbal cues, such as body language and tone of voice, during communication. By being attuned to these cues, entrepreneurs can better interpret and respond to the underlying emotions and needs of others, enhancing empathy and fostering effective communication.

c. Cultivating Empathy: Mindfulness practices support the development of empathy—the ability to understand and share the feelings of others. By cultivating empathy, entrepreneurs can connect on a deeper level with clients, employees, and partners, fostering trust, collaboration, and positive relationships.

d. Non-Violent Communication: Non-violent communication (NVC) is a communication framework that emphasizes empathy, active listening, and clear expression of needs and feelings. By integrating NVC principles with mindfulness, entrepreneurs can create a compassionate and collaborative communication style that builds stronger connections.

Cultivating Meaningful Connections and Collaborations in Business

Meaningful connections and collaborations are essential for the success of entrepreneurial ventures. Mindfulness practices offer approaches to cultivate these relationships:

a. Authenticity and Transparency: Mindfulness encourages entrepreneurs to be authentic and transparent in their interactions. By showing up genuinely and sharing openly, entrepreneurs can foster trust and build meaningful connections with others.

b. Deepening Interpersonal Connection: Mindfulness practices deepen interpersonal connection by cultivating qualities such as presence, curiosity, and compassion. By being fully present and engaged in interactions, entrepreneurs can foster meaningful connections that go beyond superficial exchanges.

c. Active Networking: Mindfulness can transform networking into a mindful and purposeful practice. By approaching networking events with genuine curiosity, active listening, and a focus on building meaningful connections, entrepreneurs can forge valuable relationships that support their business endeavors.

d. Collaboration and Team Building: Mindfulness practices enhance collaboration and team building by fostering a sense of shared purpose and empathy within teams. By practicing mindful communication, encouraging diverse perspectives, and valuing contributions, entrepreneurs can create a collaborative culture that fosters innovation and productivity.

e. Nurturing Relationships: Mindfulness reminds entrepreneurs to invest time and energy in nurturing existing relationships. By expressing gratitude, offering support, and maintaining open lines of communication, entrepreneurs can cultivate long-term connections that contribute to business growth and success.

In this chapter we emphasize on the importance of effective communication and building strong relationships in entrepreneurship. By enhancing communication skills through mindful listening, empathy, and non-violent communication, entrepreneurs can foster meaningful connections. Through authenticity, presence, and collaboration, entrepreneurs can create a network of supportive relationships that contribute to their personal and professional growth, as well as the success of their business ventures.

Chapter 9: Mindful Leadership: Inspiring and Empowering Others

We will delve into the realm of mindful leadership and explore the integration of mindfulness into leadership practices. We will emphasize the importance of becoming a mindful leader who inspires and empowers others, fostering a positive and productive work environment.

Integrating Mindfulness into Leadership Practices

Mindful leadership involves incorporating mindfulness principles and practices into one's leadership style. By integrating mindfulness into leadership practices, leaders can cultivate self-awareness, empathy, and a sense of presence. Here's how leaders can integrate mindfulness into their leadership:

a. Self-Awareness: Mindful leaders prioritize self-awareness, developing an understanding of their own thoughts, emotions, and behaviors. By cultivating self-awareness through mindfulness practices, leaders can identify and manage their biases, triggers, and strengths, enabling them to lead authentically and make conscious decisions.

b. Emotional Intelligence: Mindful leadership emphasizes emotional intelligence—the ability to understand and manage one's emotions and effectively connect with others' emotions. By cultivating emotional intelligence through mindfulness, leaders can foster a positive work environment, build strong relationships, and inspire trust and collaboration.

c. Ethical Decision-Making: Mindful leaders make decisions that align with their values and ethical principles. By integrating mindfulness into decision-making processes, leaders can develop a heightened sense of discernment, considering the broader impact of their decisions on stakeholders and the environment.

d. Mindful Communication: Mindful leaders prioritize effective and compassionate communication. By practicing mindful listening, non-judgment, and clear expression, leaders can foster open dialogue, promote understanding, and resolve conflicts in a constructive manner.

Becoming a Mindful Leader Who Inspires and Motivates Teams

Mindful leaders have the ability to inspire and empower their teams, fostering a positive and productive work environment. Here are some ways leaders can become mindful leaders who inspire and motivate their teams:

a. Leading by Example: Mindful leaders model the behaviors they wish to see in their teams. By embodying mindfulness and leading with integrity, leaders inspire others to embrace mindfulness and adopt positive work habits.

b. Cultivating a Shared Vision: Mindful leaders engage their teams in the process of creating a shared vision and purpose. By involving team members in the vision-setting process, leaders foster a sense of ownership and motivation, enabling individuals to align their work with the larger goals of the organization.

c. Nurturing Growth and Development: Mindful leaders prioritize the growth and development of their team members. By providing coaching, feedback, and opportunities for learning, leaders empower individuals to reach their full potential and contribute their unique talents to the organization.

d. Practicing Empathy and Compassion: Mindful leaders cultivate empathy and compassion towards their team members. By understanding and acknowledging the emotions and needs of individuals, leaders create a supportive and inclusive work environment that nurtures well-being and fosters collaboration.

e. Promoting Work-Life Integration: Mindful leaders recognize the importance of work-life integration and support their team members in maintaining a healthy balance. By encouraging self-care, respecting boundaries, and promoting flexibility, leaders help create an environment that values well-being and promotes sustainable high performance.

We have emphasized the significance of mindful leadership and the integration of mindfulness into leadership practices. By cultivating self-awareness, emotional intelligence, and ethical decision-making, leaders can inspire and empower their teams. Through mindful communication, leading by example, and promoting growth and well-being, leaders foster a positive work environment that encourages innovation, collaboration, and overall organizational success.

Chapter 10: Sustaining Growth and Resilience

This chapter explores the vital topic of sustaining growth and resilience in the entrepreneurial journey. It highlights the cultivation of a growth mindset and resilience through meditation, and emphasizes overcoming setbacks, learning from failures, and embracing growth opportunities.

Cultivating a Growth Mindset and Resilience through Meditation

A growth mindset and resilience are essential qualities for sustaining growth and navigating challenges in entrepreneurship. Meditation practices provide valuable tools for cultivating these qualities. Here's how meditation can support the development of a growth mindset and resilience:

a. Shifting Perspective: Meditation helps entrepreneurs shift from a fixed mindset to a growth mindset. By observing thoughts and beliefs without attachment or judgment, entrepreneurs can challenge self-limiting beliefs, embrace a mindset of continuous learning and improvement, and see setbacks as opportunities for growth.

b. Embracing Impermanence: Meditation encourages the recognition of impermanence—the understanding that everything is constantly changing. By cultivating this awareness, entrepreneurs can adapt more easily to unforeseen circumstances, overcome obstacles, and approach challenges with greater resilience and flexibility.

c. Developing Emotional Regulation: Meditation practices, such as mindfulness meditation, enhance emotional regulation skills. By observing emotions with non-judgmental awareness, entrepreneurs can develop the ability to navigate difficult emotions, respond rather than react, and make conscious decisions even in challenging situations.

d. Cultivating Self-Compassion: Meditation fosters self-compassion—a sense of kindness, understanding, and acceptance towards oneself. By cultivating self-compassion, entrepreneurs can respond to setbacks and failures with self-care, resilience, and an attitude of learning and growth.

Overcoming Setbacks, Learning from Failures, and Embracing Growth Opportunities

In the entrepreneurial journey, setbacks, failures, and growth opportunities are inevitable. Here's how entrepreneurs can navigate these experiences:

a. Embracing a Learning Mindset: Entrepreneurs can approach setbacks and failures as valuable learning experiences. By reframing these experiences as opportunities for growth and improvement, entrepreneurs can extract lessons, adjust strategies, and bounce back with renewed determination.

b. Practicing Reflection and Adaptation: Mindful reflection enables entrepreneurs to assess their experiences, identify areas for improvement, and adapt their approaches. By regularly reflecting on successes and failures, entrepreneurs can refine their strategies and make informed decisions for sustainable growth.

c. Building a Support Network: Surrounding oneself with a supportive network of mentors, peers, and advisors is crucial for overcoming setbacks and embracing growth opportunities. Collaborating with others, seeking guidance, and learning from their experiences can provide valuable insights and support during challenging times.

d. Cultivating Resilience: Resilience is the ability to bounce back and thrive in the face of adversity. Through mindfulness practices, entrepreneurs can develop resilience by strengthening their capacity to adapt, manage stress, and maintain a positive mindset. Resilience enables entrepreneurs to persevere, remain focused, and embrace growth opportunities with confidence.

e. Embracing Growth Mindset Principles: Entrepreneurs can adopt growth mindset principles such as embracing challenges, persisting in the face of setbacks, valuing effort and perseverance, seeking feedback and constructive criticism, and finding inspiration in the success of others. These principles foster a mindset that supports continuous growth and development.

We have emphasized the cultivation of a growth mindset and resilience to sustain growth in the entrepreneurial journey. Through meditation practices, entrepreneurs can develop the ability to overcome setbacks, learn from failures, and embrace growth opportunities with a sense of adaptability, learning, and determination. By integrating these qualities into their entrepreneurial mindset, entrepreneurs can navigate challenges, foster sustainable growth, and achieve long-term success.

Conclusion

This book has explored various aspects of mindful entrepreneurship, providing insights and techniques to support entrepreneurs in their journey. We began by defining mindful entrepreneurship and exploring its benefits, highlighting the integration of meditation with business practices. Throughout the chapters, we covered cultivating mindfulness, enhancing awareness and focus, managing stress and embracing uncertainty, decision-making and intuition, work-life integration, effective communication and relationship building, mindful leadership, and sustaining growth and resilience.

By incorporating mindfulness practices, entrepreneurs can enhance their self-awareness, focus, and decision-making abilities. They can manage stress, embrace uncertainty, and maintain a healthy work-life balance. Mindfulness also supports effective communication, building meaningful connections, and inspiring and empowering others as mindful leaders. Additionally, it cultivates a growth mindset, resilience, and the ability to learn from setbacks and embrace growth opportunities.

As entrepreneurs embrace mindful practices, they have the opportunity to not only create successful businesses but also foster well-being, authenticity, and compassion within themselves and their teams. Mindful entrepreneurship is about integrating mindfulness into all aspects of the entrepreneurial journey, promoting conscious decision-making, sustainable growth, and the development of positive relationships and organizational cultures.

By incorporating the principles and practices discussed in this book, entrepreneurs can embark on a journey of self-discovery, personal growth, and business success. By embracing mindfulness, entrepreneurs can create a more fulfilling and purpose-driven entrepreneurial experience while positively impacting their teams, stakeholders, and society at large. Mindful entrepreneurship offers a pathway to success that goes beyond financial achievements and encourages holistic well-being and a positive impact on the world.